Cats and Their Women

Emily Cobb and the Marblehead Kitty   PHOTO: Emily Bullard Cobb

Cats and Their Women

Barbara Cohen
and Louise Taylor

LITTLE, BROWN AND COMPANY

BOSTON   TORONTO   LONDON

Library of Congress Cataloging-in-Publication Data
Cohen, Barbara, 1949–
    Cats and their women /Barbara Cohen and Louise Taylor. — 1st ed.
        p.   cm.
    ISBN 0-316-15046-0
    1. Cats — Anecdotes.   2. Women cat owners — Anecdotes.   3. Cats —
Pictorial works.   4. Women cat owners — Pictorial works.
I. Taylor, Louise, 1949–   II. Title.
SF445.5.C62   1992
636.8 — dc20   91-31326

10   9   8   7   6   5   4   3   2   1

RRD-VA
Published simultaneously in Canada
by Little, Brown & Company (Canada) Limited

Printed in the United States of America

In memory of
Bentley, Eros, and Chamie

Acknowledgments

WE ARE EXTREMELY GRATEFUL to the hundreds of women who sent photographs, stories, and heartfelt letters to us about their cats. Their willingness to share their love for their cats with us made *Cats and Their Women* possible. We wish to also thank the photographers who patiently waited for the perfect cat moment. Many thanks to Pam White and Paula Josa-Jones for the flyer photo that got the project off to a swift and enthusiastic start. Thanks, too, to Margie Arnold for her photographs and her spirit, which kept us buoyant throughout the project.

For their assistance and support, we also wish to thank our parents Penny and Tiger Taylor, and Minna and Aaron Cohen, as well as Carol Ross, Chris Triebert, Lorrie Webb, Maggie Leduc, Marilyn Bodnar, Kathleen Marden, Kitty Reynolds, Susan Solomon, Ellie Baker, Dyhanna Noble, Eleanor Bristol, Elizabeth Malloy, Rosemary Hynes, Amy Kohut, and Suzy Becker. Special thanks to Little, Brown and Company and especially Jennifer Josephy and Alice Ma.

In the midst of working on the book, Floy Morway guided us with the care of a beautiful stray who appeared on our doorstep in the cold of winter. And Ann Marquardt found her a loving home.

The following organizations helped spread the news about the book project: the Animal Rescue League of Boston, the Delta Society, Sandra Braverman of the *Boston Globe, Animal Writes News, Art Calendar, B.V.A.U. News, South End News, Tufts Criterion, Endicott Alumni News, Cat Fancy,* and the Museum of Fine Arts School.

Last but not least, thanks to Chamie and Coopie for just being themselves, and to our dogs Gabe and Glory, who agreed to give the cats a chance with their own book.

Barbara Cohen and Coopie,
Louise Taylor and Chamie

PHOTO: Margie Arnold

Introduction

Wʜɪʟᴇ ᴡᴏʀᴋɪɴɢ on our first book, *Dogs and Their Women*, we were deluged with requests from cat lovers to write a similar book depicting the loving relationship between women and cats. Inspired by the enthusiasm and encouragement we received, we started planning for *Cats and Their Women* not long after *Dogs and Their Women* was published in 1989. Cats, like dogs, play a major role in many women's lives, and this we felt deserved to be celebrated as well.

Through nationwide cat publications and organizations, we began soliciting unique stories and photographs of women with their cats. While we received well over 600 photographs, we hadn't anticipated how difficult it would be to take photographs of cats and women together. Cats didn't like flash bulbs or cameras, they didn't like to be held, and they were usually afraid of the photographer. Cats, it seemed, didn't want anything to do with this book.

Accompanying us on our quest for the most unusual and touching photographs of cats and their women were our own cats Chamie and Coopie, two of the most unlikely candidates for this book. Who would be interested in a fat old tabby whose stomach practically touches the ground when she walks, and a scrawny, unfriendly, seemingly unremarkable white cat? Whether sleeping beside the computer or sprawled next to a stack of cat photographs and stories, however, Chamie and Coopie were our muses. They were constant reminders that this book is about everyday cats and women, coming together to play, to make sure everyone is fed on time, for the sweet sound of purring, and, most important, for unconditional love.

In the following pages you'll meet Holly Baldwin and Bud, who bridge their separate worlds through sign language, and Norma Marinelli, who saved Li'l Red from a near-fatal accident on a Mississippi River barge. The triumphs of pet therapy are told by Joan Bernstein, whose cats not only rescued her from terrible bouts of chronic fatigue immune dysfunction syndrome but "unlocked a whole new world, and a wonderful new career" for her. Listen to four-year-old Emily Marsters tell the story of her first cat, Tippy. Hear how Cheryl Lichak rescued sixteen-year-old Oliver, "toothless, torn, and tattered." Meet the kitty named Pup, who lives with the pup named Kitty, and Inky, a smart cat in a correctional institution who manages to get fed around the clock.

Cats and Their Women comes from cities and country towns all across America. Everywhere — even as alarm clocks become superfluous, trophies of dead mice proliferate, and favorite armchairs are compromised — the love that women have for their cats reigns supreme.

Cats and Their Women

THESE are my babies, Rose and Tessie. I had only intended on getting one gray kitten, but Tessie with her little ginger face came prancing along and stole my heart.

Tessie hunts insects. She likes the flavor of moths and flies. Rose is the shy one. She's the hunter of the family and brings all kinds of small wild things through her cat door. I've had to catch chipmunks, a bunny, a baby squirrel, moles, birds, and even a bat. I'm getting very skilled at catching mice in a widemouth plastic cup. I'm thinking of tagging them to see if the same mice are getting recaptured!

PHOTO: Margie Arnold

Linda Granger with Rose and Tessie

THIS IS MY BEST BUD, Bud. He's beautiful, full of personality, and a character! He loves to scan the ceiling for flies when I pick him up, and he gets along well with the three other cats at my house.

Bud is special because he's deaf. I taught him sign language — he looks for me when I flash the lights, and his name, in signing, is wiggling fingers!

It's funny to think I didn't need to name him, since he'll never hear me call his name.

PHOTO: Sarah Baldwin

Holly Baldwin and Bud

At the time Tootie came to live with me, I was still grieving for the loss of my dearly loved cat Minou, who had disappeared. The loss was made even more painful because of the uncertainty of what happened to her.

Tootie seemed like a miracle. Young though she was, she seemed to know that I needed to be comforted and she proceeded to take care of me just as Minou had done.

When I am in the garden on my hands and knees, weeding and planting, Tootie likes to come and help me. If I dig a hole, she pushes the earth back before I can get a plant in it! She thinks bulbs are a special kind of fun ball for her to play with and scatters them all over the place if I take more than one at a time out of the bag.

My favorite chair is her favorite chair, so we compromise. If she is there first, I sit somewhere else. Last week Tootie took off and was gone for twenty-four hours. When she finally returned, my life began again.

Photo: Russell Mott II

Joan Watson and Tootie

WHEN CASHMERE WAS PREGNANT, her small frame swelled, nearly tripling in poundage, and lumpy protrusions appeared on her sides. I called her extra masses "Lump" and "Bump" and decided a third arrival, though it wasn't expected, would be "Thump." If a fourth appeared, it certainly would be a "Surprise."

On the night that Cashmere went into labor, she kept me up all night rubbing, poking, and pushing against me. She'd roll across me on her back and push her paws into my chin as I rubbed her aching belly. When I did doze off, she insistently pressed her face against my mouth or meowed right into my ear to rouse me. Sure enough, Cashmere, never one to disappoint, produced four kittens.

Audrey L. D. Petschek with Cashmere,
Lump, Bump, Thump, and Surprise

PHOTO: Betty J. Petschek

Having a cat while living in a third-floor condo was the furthest thing from my mind. I had become used to living alone, no one to think about but myself. That was soon to change. On several occasions in the fall of 1989, upon arriving home, I found a black cat with big green eyes settled on the scatter rug in front of my door. How she got through so many doors to get there still puzzles me. Thinking she must belong to someone, I would pick her up and put her outside. She was not about to give up. On Saturday, the eighteenth of November, I left in the morning to do my weekly grocery shopping and other errands. As I was leaving the parking lot, I had to come to a sudden stop so I wouldn't run over a black cat running from the dumpster area. When I arrived home about three P.M., to my surprise, there was the black cat sleeping in front of my door. As I struggled with the groceries after opening the door, in walked the black cat as though she had always lived there. You guessed it: back to the store to buy cat food, litter, and toys, as I figured she was here to stay.

It is still a mystery why, out of 336 units, she picked mine.

PHOTO: Photography by Kristen,
Stow, Massachusetts

Phyllis Priest and Misty

CASPER is the youngest member of what my grandmother likes to call my "cat collection," which presently includes four felines. I did not discover that Casper was aquatic until I began to take frequent bubble baths to alleviate my aches and pains from long cycling treks.

When Casper hears the water running in the bathroom, he comes in and parks himself on the bath mat. When I get in the tub, he jumps on the edge and roams up and down, occasionally stopping to stick his paw into the bubbles, wash himself, or, much to his surprise, pull his long tail out of the water.

Casper seems to defy the rules of nature, well, at least cat nature, with his aquatic tendencies. I think he's really a catfish.

Jean Canfield and Casper

It was April 1988 at Friar Point on the Mississippi River. We were loading a soybean barge at the McAlister Grain Company. As Big John was moving the last 5,000 bushels onto the barge, a bright orange ball of fur tumbled out of the conveyor pipe into the barge. He recognized it at once as my cat Li'l Red. Li'l Red was born at the elevator several years earlier. He was extremely wild with any human except me. The men would occasionally catch a glimpse of an orange streak, but all Li'l Red's love was reserved for me.

As soon as Big John saw Li'l Red, he radioed to the men to cut off the conveyor belts and notify me at once. I ran out of the office, down the riverbank, across the gangplank, and onto the barge in my three-inch heels and with my skirt hiked way above my knees. I lowered myself into the barge and, within seconds, found myself knee-deep in soybeans. I lay on my stomach and could see Li'l Red lying against the side of the barge. With every move I made, the soybeans shifted and covered him a little more. I was past panicking. If I didn't get him out, he would suffocate.

For the next hour, as I calmly talked to Li'l Red, I used my hands to shovel some of the soybeans that were between me and him to the men who were standing by on top of the barge. I had Jodi find a cardboard box and my jacket. Once I grabbed Li'l Red, he would have to be covered or he would bolt from my arms as soon as he saw someone else. Finally, I lunged head-first toward Li'l Red. I grabbed him by his back legs just as he was sinking deeper into the barge. The soybeans shifted and began covering both of us. The men reacted quickly and pulled me and Li'l Red out by my legs.

When I finally got my head out of the barge and stopped to take a breath of air, all the men were standing on the barge clapping, and the entire office staff was on the riverbank doing the same. I was so proud and excited. I loved all of them for their help and support, because they knew how much Li'l Red meant to me.

Photo: Lindsay Reid

Norma Marinelli and Li'l Red

YOU'RE WONDERING why a dog is in this story about cats? It's okay, her name is Kitty. From this you can guess what I call one of my four cats. That's right — Pup.

Kitty, the dog, loves to get the cats to lick her face with their raspy tongues. She sticks her head down in front of one of them, and somehow they know what she wants. Pup will lick her the longest amount of time — for several minutes. Tara will only grant a few licks and walk away. Rags is downright insulted she's asked, refusing even to stick her tongue out. Izzy starts to lick, but then, adolescent that she is, turns it into more of a biting and playing event.

A house without pets? I can't imagine anyone denying themselves the fun and comfort that these amusing characters bring.

PHOTO: Ervand Peterson

Judie Westenberg-Peterson with Pup,
Tara, Wragby, Izzy, and Kitty the dog

WINNIE, a tiny kitten, was found discarded like garbage near a laundry room. She was filthy, her eyes, ears, and mouth packed with greasy dirt, and so cold to the touch that at first we thought she was dead.

Winnie is four years old now, and she's overcome enormous odds. Her problems are probably attributable to those traumatic first few weeks of life. There is very little grace to Winnie; the seemingly effortless leaps onto high places or across long distances that we take for granted in cats are beyond her. Her misaligned right eye makes her depth perception unreliable, and she exhibits a marked hesitation before as simple an act as jumping onto the bed or my lap. She is small, barely eight pounds, and walks with an ungainly plodding gait, often staggering, especially after a nap. Yet for all of this, Winnie is one of the most affectionate, sweet-natured cats that I have had the fortune to befriend.

Susan Jones and Winnie

SPENSER WAS A GIFT at a time in my life when I needed his warm, tender spirit. He has the smallest body, the largest ears, and an even larger, loving heart. He is a source of comfort and joy — the kind of companion you know will come along only once in a lifetime.

PHOTO: Pam White

Ann Briley and Spenser

My EXPERIENCES as an army nurse with the 56th Evacuation Hospital (5th Army Corps) are just memories now. It was a good time in my life, in spite of the hardships. Now, after many years of caring for people, I enjoy my days on the farm with my cat Cyrus. It is a peaceful life. Cyrus is three years old and sleeps on my bed most of the time. A few times, when I went out to the chicken house to let the chickens out in the morning, I found Cyrus asleep with them.

When Cyrus wants to come in the house, he sits on the window ledge outside by the dog kennel so all our dogs can see him. When the dogs bark at Cyrus, I know that he wants to be let in the house. If I don't let him in right away, the dogs won't be quiet. I think Cyrus is a very smart cat.

PHOTO: Sister Pauline Quinn

Frances Robb and Cyrus

Each one of the cats surrounding me has a story of its own. One was found on a cold, rainy day this winter in the bottom of an empty dumpster. He was half dead from hypothermia and starvation. After twenty-four hours on a heating pad in front of a wood stove, he recovered and joined the "group."

Last Chance was about to be put to sleep for lack of a home. Henuan, a very relaxed cat, came with BB pellets imbedded in his hindquarters. But there are many happy stories here also. Those who are not adoptable just stay on.

Photo: Judith Hoch

Floy Morway with cats

A YEAR AGO, my husband, Ted, was in the hospital critically ill. It was the first time I faced the reality that he could die.

After spending three days and nights at the hospital, I took a break and went home. I needed to see Socrates and tell him everything that was going through my mind — things I couldn't say to family or friends for fear of upsetting them. I told him how desperately scared I was that things would never be the same for us and that we would be alone. I held him so close.

I truly believe he helped me find the strength to go through the most difficult struggle of my life.

PHOTO: On Location Photography
Topsfield, Massachusetts

Nancy Moore and Socrates

MY LOVE for cats started about the age of ten. I saw Joan Embery with a tiger cub on the Carson show, and I knew then I had to train big cats. Instead of running away to the circus, I went to college: Moorpark College Exotic Animal Training and Management Program.

After several different jobs I was hired as head trainer for a three-month engagement in Lake Tahoe. Two weeks before the end of that engagement, my life changed forever. My boss bought a three-week-old black leopard, and I was given the job of raising her. That meant five baby bottles of formula a day and lots of laundry. Having a baby leopard living in a small apartment was a lot of work — she was into everything! She shredded paper towels and chewed through the telephone cord numerous times. Her favorite place to sleep was the bathroom sink. She learned to ride a skateboard at work, and she still has a love for her skateboard today.

Prudence turned three years old in August 1991. With her help, someday I wish to build a compound to raise and breed endangered species, like the clouded leopard and the snow leopard. Animal training is not an abusive job; it can be done humanely, with love and affection. My whole life is dedicated to animals. As all cat and animal lovers in this book and in the world would agree, there is something unique about the unconditional love that animals bring into your life.

PHOTO: Steve Pratt   *Nicolienne Francois and Prudence (black leopard)*

COLLECTIVELY CALLED THE BOYS, Spenser and Simon act in tandem to accomplish their mission. Often the goal of their game is for both of them to occupy the same spot on my lap at the same time. During our nightly reading sessions, their strategy has to include overcoming the book barrier. However, they have me nicely conditioned to move the book outward, leaving room for Simon, the larger of the two, to snuggle in, and for Spenser, the wiser of the two, to lie on top of Simon. Moving them is out of the question! Don't even suggest it!

PHOTO: Pam White

Edna Ward with Simon and Spenser

MY THREE CATS, Pasha, Lucifer, and Keeley, seemed to sense that today was going to be a hectic one. My wedding gown looked beautiful! At the bottom left sat the hand-beaded cat I had designed to match the beading on the rest of my dress. The cat would be evident as I walked — I wanted a cat somewhere with me on my wedding day.

When the photographer arrived, I said that I had to have several pictures taken with my cats. When my father brought Lucy into the living room, she just about shredded his tuxedo, and he declared that Pasha wouldn't be much better. But Keeley, who was curious about everything, was found sniffing inside the photographer's camera bag. She seemed a willing participant.

I sat on the floor, attempting to get Keeley's attention. I shook my bouquet and she made a jump for — what else — the pussy willows. Since my dress was spread out on the carpeted floor, Keeley was right up on it. The photographer started to have a fit about Keeley catching the dress with her needlelike claws. Keeley did tear my lace gloves, but only I would know. The photographer continued shooting and then announced she had time for one last shot.

It's as though Keeley understood, and as I bent over to tell her what a little angel she was, her face came right up to mine and her wee nose and mouth pressed against my lips. It was so touching I had to fight back the tears. At that moment I felt that nothing would go wrong that day.

PHOTO: Amora Portrait Studio
Mississauga, Ontario

Elizabeth White Norheim and Keeley

THROUGHOUT THE SUMMER, I would only have to call once and a furry ball of black and white would come running from behind the building of the music company where I work. Mitch Miller knew the voice meant breakfast. He had a funny-looking black goatee beneath his white mouth, and he was friendly for a stray, even letting me pet him. With winter approaching, I decided to bring this personable little guy inside. As friendly as he was, however, Mitch Miller would have no part in being picked up or brought inside. He squirmed, clawed, and eventually ran away at each of my attempts. This went on for about two months.

On a particularly cold, rainy December day, I could no longer bear to think of him outside. I made a plan and enlisted the help of my friend Richard. With gloves on, I would quickly catch Mitch Miller and deposit him into a box. Richard would close the lid. We had to work fast — I did not know if I would ever get another chance.

We were both ready. I called Mitch Miller, and as usual, he came running. As he was eating, we waited for the right moment to put the plan into action. He finished and was looking quite content. "Now!" I heard myself shout, and had him in my hands. I waited for him to squirm and claw me to death. To my surprise, he was calm and collected. I dropped him in the box, and Richard gently closed the lid. One meow was all we heard. Loosely translated, I think he was saying, "Baby, it's cold outside!"

PHOTO: Jeff Martin   *Pearl Lee and Mitch Miller*

Although he is a mixed breed, I named him Sir Charles because of his regal appearance as a kitten. He has, however, become known as Charley since the name better suits his gentle, sweet-natured personality.

Melissa Hale Spence and Charley

"THE GIRLS" (Rita Mae and Minnie Pearl) are two little sisters who are sometimes my snugglebugs and sometimes little monster cats. They like to bite my toes at night, play trapeze artist on the clothesline, and steal my stuffed bunny.

Rita has a fondness for bananas. She carries them around in her teeth until they're bruised and half peeled.

Minnie, who started out as the squeaky runt of the litter, is usually a bit more dignified — until she goes absolutely crazy playing in the spray of the humidifier or with a new toy mouse. She's also an expert at looking so cute you'll give her anything she wants . . . but both of them have quite a talent for that.

Angela Beauchamp with Rita Mae and Minnie Pearl

Spot is my best buddy. We spend every day together making pots while discussing art and food. Every day ends up the same. We eat tuna fish and he tells me to put more cats on my pots.

Photo: Fritz Lauenstein

June Rita Raymond and Spot

LULU IS AN ORDINARY CAT. She doesn't aim to please. She doesn't enter-
tain or humor me. Lulu is pure and simple, and just as endearing as any
feline housemate I've shared my life with over the years.

PHOTO: Maggie Miller

Itati' and Lulu

DIANA AND I have been together for nine years, since I found her as a kitten at an ice cream store. She was on her way to the pound with her mother and siblings, but she clung to me and meowed loudly anytime someone tried to take her off my lap.

I am paralyzed totally with a muscle disease. At that time I could still move my right hand some. Although I have total feeling, I could not lift or move Diana. She used to help me lift my hand with her head so that I could pet her. Now that I have no more use of that hand except for some thumb movement, she pets me by moving her head against my hand or face. My lap is her kingdom. She rides with me on my electric wheelchair, and sometimes she lies on my chest and cuddles up against me as I rest. When my attendant lifts my hand onto Diana's head, Diana will remain perfectly still while my hand stays balanced on her head and I pet her by wiggling my thumb.

She often sits by and watches as I do my daily routine and respiratory therapy, purring and winking at me the whole time. Diana is psychic. Many women have spirit guides. Diana seems to be mine.

Connie Panzarino and Diana

TIFFANY ARRIVED on my seventh wedding anniversary, the day after Thanksgiving. I went outside to enjoy the autumn leaves and suddenly at my feet appeared a gray orphan kitten. I took her inside the house and bathed her. Much to my surprise, the gray fur turned out to be white. She then perched herself against the wedding picture in my bedroom and would not move.

Three years have passed. Tiffany has joined my other cats and is a real joy. When it is nap time I know where to find her. She is always sleeping next to my wedding photo.

PHOTO: T. G. McCary Photography

Susan Callon and Tiffany

MY NAME IS EMILY and I had a cat named Tippy. We got Tippy in Sudbury, Massachusetts. We picked her out from a few other kittens. Tippy was the most cute. She was white, gray, and black. Right after we got her, we got a flea collar, then when we got back home we gave her a flea bath. She didn't like that. When she was still a kitten, I took her for a ride in the doll carriage. Sometimes I wrapped her up in a blanket! She loved that. Sometimes my sister and I would dress her up in baby clothes. Sometimes she slept with me; I loved it when she did. When she was two years, she had two babies. When we had them, me and my sister each had one. Their names kept changing! One was named Snowflake for a while. We gave the one that I was taking care of to one of my friends. We gave my sister's to her friend. The second time Tippy was going to have babies her tummy was very full. We were at my grandparents' for the day. When we came home at nighttime my dad saw a cat lying down on the side of the road very near our house. He didn't know if it was our cat or our neighbor's cat, so we went and looked and it was our cat, so we said good-bye and my dad buried her and we all cried and went to bed. We buried her in a box with a pillow and a blanket. And now we have a cat named Frisky.

PHOTO: Margie Arnold

Emily Marsters, four, and Tippy

KIZZIE is my No. 1 Tonkinese co-therapist; Dovey is second only to Kizzie with one exception: Little Moth, the shoulder cat everyone adores. Kiz is particularly adept with profoundly handicapped people of all ages. When atrophied or missing limbs prevent a person from fondling Kiz, she simply finds a perch on the person's midsection, tucks her head under their chin, and does the job herself. If they don't respond, she encourages them vocally until they do. Her voice isn't as harsh as a Siamese, but she can get extremely insistent!

Dovey prefers men, especially those prone in bed or geriatric chairs. Once he's under an afghan or in the crook of an elbow, he's an immovable object. Dovey's clients reap the full benefit of our Cat Assisted Therapy Service. He would love it if we arrived before dinner and stayed until breakfast time. Not Moth. She's much too busy flitting from client to client, enticing youngsters and elderly alike to play. It doesn't matter if the hand holding her stick toy is gnarled and arthritic, weak and fumbling. One electively mute young man, who signed "cat" for a year of visits, finally said his first complete word to Moth: "Cat!"

When Kiz is on maternity leave, or Dov is feeling slightly burned out, Little Brother, Cinnamonbred, Kira, Magpye, Remember, Fame, Cachet, Tayglech, or Ducky, to name a few of the human-bonded Tonkinese I use in my programs, have their turns. Fame is the first cat a severely phobic autistic youngster ever touched. We swear Fame mesmerized Page, compelling him from his safe spot on the stairs across the room to sit next to this twelve-pound platinum mink male cat. Once he established eye contact with the boy (often a breakthrough with autistics), Fame never let go.

During my worst sieges of chronic fatigue immune dysfunction syndrome, my cats still had to be cared for. They challenged the pain, fatigue, physical dysfunction, disorientation, and depression. They won. They unlocked a whole new world, and a wonderful new career for me.

Joan Bernstein with Certified Therapy Cats,
Kizzie, Dovey, and Moth

PHOTO: Marilyn Lehrfeld

WE WERE born in different places, Turtle and I, she in the Vermont woods, without people, and I in a New York suburb, without a cat. But early in her life she ventured onto the deck outside our kitchen in Shaftsbury, Vermont. Here she ate our kibble, leaned into our caresses, and began to stay, settling her roundness onto the deck and staring out over the Green Mountains and in through our kitchen door. Four years later, when she was sure she could trust us, she came inside. She was five then, and she hasn't spent a night outside in the ten years since.

But she has been on the cover of a book (my *Maverick Cats: Encounters with Feral Cats*) and her story helped to focus attention on cats gone wild around the world. She knows nothing of the personal letters, the little gifts, the serious reviews from people she never met. She only knows what she needs to know, and undoubtedly this doesn't include the legend in some parts of the British Isles that it is a good omen when a tortoiseshell cat settles in the house. And what do I know, beyond books and legends and such things? That Turtle is special beyond any of that.

PHOTO: Roy Berkeley

Ellen Perry Berkeley and Turtle

I WAS A FIRST-YEAR VETERINARY STUDENT and frequented the Tuskegee Small Animal Clinic. One of the clinicians had talked me into adopting not one but two kittens.

I picked up Frost and gave him to a classmate to carry to the car. I reached for the female, Sister Cat (the name I shall call her), and the fun started. She spat and ran to the farthest corner of the cage, and Shannan, a third kitty, meowed and jumped into my arms. I told her no, I couldn't adopt three cats, and pushed her back. I tried to grab Sister Cat, who was hissing and turning into a Halloween rendition for a cat poster. Shannan decided she was not going to be left and proceeded to get my attention by clinging to my shirtfront with all four paws. Meanwhile I was trying to grab Sister Cat, who was swatting at me. During this time, the person who was giving me a ride home showed up and said she had to leave. Frustrated, I gave up Sister Cat, grabbed Shannan (who started purring up a storm), and took her home.

Bringing Shannan home turned out to be one of the best things I ever did. She has helped make the pathway to being a veterinarian a little easier by enriching my life with her antics and giving me firsthand experience in feline behavior. She provides constant companionship and never faults me (even after I adopted two dogs), never holds a grudge (even when her dinner is four hours late due to an unexpected surgery), and is the only cat I know with a thorough knowledge of gross anatomy (learned firsthand by reading over my shoulder). She is one of my best friends, and I love her dearly.

PHOTO: Sherelle R. Williams   *Greta Walker and Shannan*

THE GIRLS run the show. They're waiting for me at the door when I get home, and after excessive Siamese caterwauling, I give in and let them go outside. I tell them to stay in the yard, but of course they don't listen. I have to get up at five A.M. to give them breakfast or else be subjected to Jada's deafening meows and Misha's Siamese Whisker Torture. I've belonged to countless animal companions over the years, but none has been as loud, demanding, bossy, intelligent, affectionate, or devoted as these two. Some people tease me about being obsessed with the girls, but I don't mind. The most important thing they've taught me so far is to go after what makes me happy. With their support, I recently decided to make the transition from biochemical research to veterinary medicine. Having Jada and Misha around has been a constant reminder of what is meaningful to me and what makes me happy.

PHOTO: Judith Hoch   *Kimberly Klaiber with Misha and Jada*

MINNA
Minolta
Minerva
Mintel
Mihitabelly
Miphistie
Minacle
Minnie
Mins
Minch
Minnie the Pooh
Mrs. Minniefur
Minnatonka
Minniehapless
Minnow
Tank

THE SOFTEST BELLY, the best sleeping companion, she moves with me, curls with me, purrs with me, shares fleas with me, tail up, the silent meow and a small squeak when I come in the door, but she's best in bed, under the covers, never know she's there until I get in, then a soft stirring and she's stretched against the small of my back or rounded into my stomach, no hint ever of her needing to sleep again, she's always ready.

PHOTO: © Paula Josa-Jones
Names by Paula Josa-Jones and Pam White

Pam White and Minna

Six months ago I learned that Cricket has lymphoma — a kind of solid tumor leukemia that has settled into her stomach. I had to make one of the most difficult decisions of my life when the veterinarians offered her chemotherapy and the possibility of another year or so of life. Having watched the slow, painful demise of humans under chemotherapeutic treatment, I was racked with indecision.

I thought about the responsibility I had accepted when I took this cat into my life, and I thought about the trust she had vested in me when we made our quiet pact. I searched for books on animal death and its ethics. Ultimately, I made the decision to treat the disease when my husband reminded me that a year is a long time in a cat's life and that our time together could be seen as a long farewell.

Our farewell has been made of the same sweet, quiet stuff that has been the foundation of our relationship.

Jane Gaughan and Cricket

PENNY was a five-week-old ball of white, orange, and black fur, in constant motion, when she first came into my life six and a half years ago.

She has grown up to be a highly intelligent, very beautiful cat — a trifle chubby, but every inch a lady. She has learned to dodge the wheels of my chair, and only once in our years together has the tip of her tail been pinched.

She has brought many happy hours into my life with her antics, and I love her dearly. I guess the sign on the back of my wheelchair sums up our relationship: "I'm in charge today, my cat said so!"

PHOTO: Linda M. Wolk

Barbara Walsh and Penny

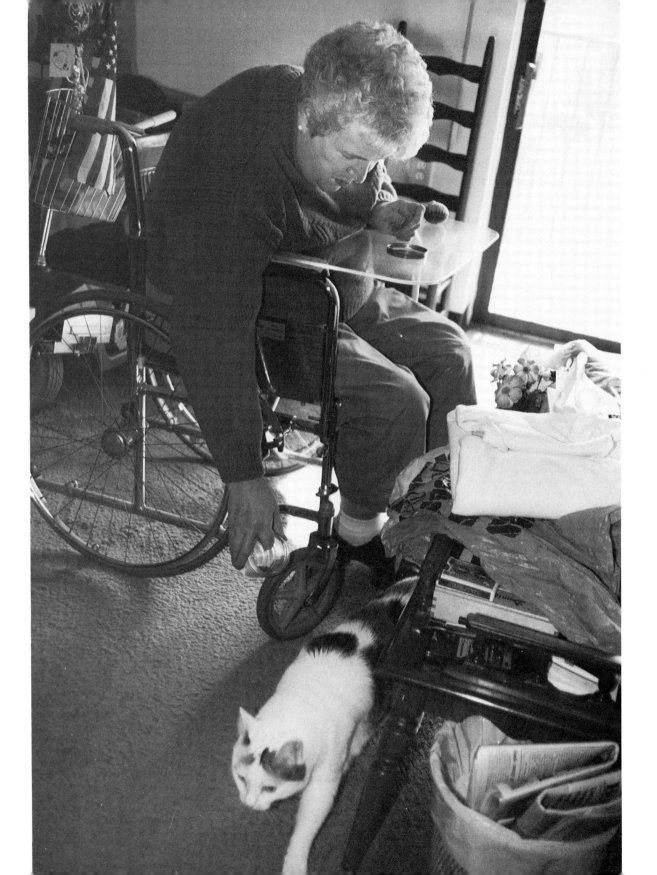

My CAT ABBEY AND I have a very special relationship. I think it came from both of us being "farm girls." I grew up on a dairy farm in Iowa and was always surrounded by hundreds of cats.

I had recently moved to a city and was bound and determined to get a cat. I had spent the day looking through papers and pet stores, when I finally came upon an ad for a Siamese kitten. I drove over hilly country roads to an old farmhouse to pick her up. There, at the bottom of a hallway closet cluttered with clothes, boots, and hats, was a basketful of cute, cuddly Siamese kittens. Since I wasn't planning to show my kitten, I took the one with a large dot marking the top of her head — Abbey Sue or, as she's affectionately known, Huggy Bunny.

I took Abbey home and she slept, protected under my arm from the big city that surrounded us. In reality, I think she was protecting me . . . from my loneliness.

Lu Ann Pettinger and Abbey Sue

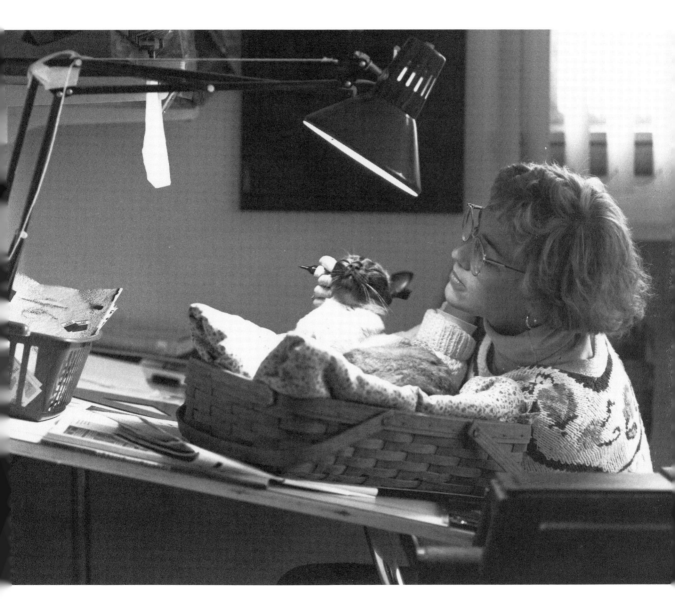

THE ALARM GOES OFF for the first time. My hand slaps the snooze button, and I flip over onto my back for another six minutes. Katiti, who has been napping on the edge of the bed, tiptoes over to my prone body, circles my head so she can smell my breath, gently steps onto my belly, and crawls up to my chest. There she settles, purring loudly, with her paws nearly on my chin. Then, as the minutes tick by, she gradually increases the decibels of her purr and stares at my eyes until they flutter open at the shriek of the alarm. Her response is simply "meow."

Kareem, waiting at the side of the bed for his accomplice to do her job, now echoes her meows, and I'm forced to get up and follow him as he lopes to the kitchen. If I stop to go to the bathroom, he'll track me down and keep meowing until I follow him to the cat food. As soon as the can is opened, Kareem jumps on top of the refrigerator to watch as his sister, the true seducer, has her fill first.

Karen Krebsbach with Kareem and Katiti

ONE AFTERNOON, as I made my way through the ward at the veterinary hospital where I worked, I came across a cat with no cage card. I could tell just by looking at him that his injuries were extensive and he was in critical condition. He had been hit by a car sometime the night before. He had no owner, and since his prognosis was very poor, we would probably only keep him for the five days required by law. If he showed no improvement and no owner was found, he would then be put to sleep.

I could not ignore this poor creature. I knew if there was any hope for his recovery, he would have to be with someone who loved him. His head injuries and broken pelvis made it difficult for him to stand, but each day Max (the name I gave him) and I made a little progress. He began eating and drinking on his own (he was a pig), was able to stand up, and even took a few steps before falling over.

When the day came for Max to be put to sleep, I just couldn't let it happen since he was making such good progress. Only one thing bothered me. Sometimes I would find him staring blankly at the back of his cage or he would hit his head on the sides of it. Through a series of simple tests, we discovered that Max was blind. Now we faced an even bigger dilemma. Who would want a blind cat? What kind of life would Max have without his sight? But I had worked too hard with him, and loved him too much, to give up on him.

Max took his blindness in stride, as he had all his other injuries, and adjusted beautifully. Many clients did not believe he was blind when they saw him walking or running through the hospital. In every way he seemed like a normal cat. When I left my position there, I could not bear to leave him behind. I was a little bit nervous about the adjustment to a new place he would have to make. Max has done well in his new apartment. He has plenty of room to run around, and he loves to play with my other cat.

Max has come a long way from that pitiful cat I saw in the cage nearly three years ago. Seeing him today, I know I made the right decision for him. He is a beautiful and healthy cat.

PHOTO: Tam Garson

Tara Martin and Max

WHEN YOU WATCH kitty litter and frozen raw meat arrive by the half ton, you know cats are important to me.

I am very involved in the breeding, raising, and showing of a breed known as the British shorthair — a wonderful, sturdy, stocky cat. My love for and adventures with my cats will last the rest of my life. They are my beloved pets first; the breeding and showing are secondary pursuits. If I were told tomorrow that all my animals had to be neutered and spayed and I could never show again, I would have some adjustments to make, but the litter and the frozen meat would still arrive by the half ton!

PHOTO: Carl J. Widmer

Dr. Ginger Meeker with Hazen,
Wellington, and Brigadoon

INKY IS THE RESIDENT PRISON CAT at the Washington Corrections Center for Women (WCCW), where the inmate population averages 300 female felons. With that many women, you can imagine that Inky is well loved and certainly well fed!

Inky was just a handful of a kitten when she was brought into the prison two years ago by one of the guards, who found her in the parking lot. As a kitten she was a real fireball, hissing, spitting, and being generally evil to everyone and everything. I've always suspected that Inky came from a litter of wild cats that lived in the woods surrounding the prison. Luckily, with constant love from me and many of the women, Inky is now a very loving cat, though she is still fiercely independent.

Inky technically lives with me, in the sense that I am responsible for her feeding, her health, and any problems she may get into. Though Inky does sleep with me most of the time, she is well known for stretching out on any of the fifty-six beds in my unit.

Inky's feeding schedule is probably unlike that of any other cat. A majority of the women keep cans of shrimp, cheese, or other tidbits that they leave out for Inky. Consequently, Inky cruises the hallway, going from room to room and eating as the urge strikes her — sort of like a smorgasbord.

One of the most unique bridges that Inky has crossed is that of the language barrier. There are several non–English speaking women at WCCW who have a tendency to be withdrawn because of the language barrier. Inky will sit down on any lap that is warm and willing. For these women, it is an opportunity to express and receive some love. A couple of the women have even come up to me, communicating through motions and signals that they like Inky, want to feed her, or are looking for her to cuddle with. Inky is the first cat I've ever had. She is without a doubt my most understanding friend — one that never judges my faults or moods — and she is always a source of joy.

PHOTO: Marsha Henkel   *Jeannette Murphy and Inky*

My NAME IS ANGIE. I was a graduation gift to my mom in May 1974. We spent our first two weeks together in her dorm at Smith College. After that we lived in Belchertown, and I had five kittens and romped in the fields. Then I became a city cat in Boston for two years. Next I was whisked away to California for nine years, where I had to support my Mom throughout graduate school. If that wasn't hard enough, she added another cat twelve years ago and a husband five years ago. I hate sharing her attention, but at least I have someone to sleep with and another lap to sit on. Five years ago, we all moved back to the Pioneer Valley. I don't like the snow, but it's nice to get back to my roots. In 1989, I celebrated Mom's fifteenth college reunion and our fifteen years together — we both thought that was pretty great. She never would have made it without me!

PHOTO: Molly Goodwin

Molly Goodwin and Angie

I HAD WANTED A CAT for a long time, and in January 1980, while living in Boulder, Colorado, I set out for the Humane Society to adopt one. I realized I had taken the wrong road when I began heading out of town, so I stopped for directions. When I asked a woman where the Humane Society was, she asked me if I wanted a cat. Her cat had had kittens and she wanted to get rid of the female as she didn't want any more kittens. We went out to the barn, where the kittens were living. We tried and tried but could not coax the female into the box. There was one kitty who showed interest, who wanted to come along. That one kitty was my little Felix. He chose me and has been my best friend ever since.

PHOTO: Kelemen

Kyle Menichetti and Felix

Morgan fills every nook and cranny of my being; wherever I am, that's where Morgan wants to be. When I'm sitting at the table typing, painting, or just having lunch, Morgan is right there too, eager to share the day's activities with me. He'll playfully butt heads with me, chatting all the while in his soft, oddly kittenlike voice, and I'll respond with the best cat sounds I can make. He doesn't scoff at my efforts to emulate his language; he has too much innate dignity for that. As I cuddle him and tell him sincerely (a cat will sense falseness) what a great cat he is, Morgan's guileless sea-green eyes slowly close and his whole body purrs. Just holding him, just savoring the beauty and warmth of his person, makes all the trials of daily living fade away. Morgan has never done anything unusual or heroic. He doesn't have to. He has given me his love, unfettered and without reservations — what more can anyone ask?

PHOTO: John Aulick

Karen Kuykendall and Morgan

My husband complains he is surrounded and outnumbered by women and cats! He's right. And he loves it.

Sarah and Bud,
Anna and Duke,
Holly and Lily, and
Rosemary and Daisy

GROWING UP in the country, my brother and I entertained ourselves most of the time, and animals were our important companions. My family had plenty of animals; one year we had seventeen cats, including kittens. We would invent stories about the cats and play them out. Two particularly obliging cats, Sally and Tommy, would allow us to dress them up to be the stars in our plays.

Sally made me her person for the entire sixteen years of her life. She watched me grow up: through the good year of a six-year-old whose biggest concern was trying to catch her to put a scarf on her head, to the not-so-good year of a sixteen-year-old who stayed alone in a room, crying about being a flat-chested, gawky girl who didn't get asked to dance. When I reached out for a consoling hug, Sally shared my worst moments and gave her unconditional love.

As Sally watched me grow up, I in turn watched her grow old. When Sally finally died, it seemed to end a part of my life.

Victoria E. McOmie and Squidgie

MICKEY had been up for adoption for at least a month. People would come into the clinic and fall for his lovable personality, but nobody took him home. He was too old, too big, too tough-looking. There was always some excuse.

I was at the clinic to put my cat Pearl to sleep. He was nineteen and a half years old. I was twelve years old when he crawled into my lap, looked up at me, and blinked. We had been together ever since.

Through my tears I saw Mickey beckoning me with a paw through the bars. I couldn't resist. I took him home the next day. The only reason I waited that long was to make sure I wasn't trying to replace Pearl. He was, of course, impossible to replace. However, his death left a horrible emptiness that only a cat could fill. I just couldn't stand being in the house without Pearl.

As soon as I brought Mickey home, I knew it was the right decision. He was so happy he didn't know what to do with himself. I swear he had never slept on a bed before. He had this look on his face of complete disbelief that anything could be that comfortable.

Today, a year later, I still miss Pearl. It still hurts. It just hurts a little less because I can look at Mickey's comical face and listen to his thunderous purr.

Go in peace, Pearl.

Katherine Reiner and Mickey

No cat was ever more aware of his importance than Max. He knew the day began, revolved around, and ended with him. Not a meal could be eaten without him presuming to sample each course, including dessert. The act of drying hair took twice as long because Max had his own hair-styling technique. Crossword puzzles had to be left unfinished, attempts to play Scrabble became hilarious disasters, and reading was hopeless. He needed to participate, touch, be the center of attention and the main attraction.

Max took the longest journey after only two years of life, and I miss him like the dickens.

Madge Bennett and Max

BIGGS has the temperament of a teddy bear. He purrs with the touch of a hand. His favorite place to sleep is his sea bunk (a shelf on the wall). From there, he watches the birds and squirrels in the big tree outside and takes bites from the spider plant overhead. He is one of the most gentle and loving cats I have ever known.

PHOTO: John August Black

Kristen Norweg and Biggs

Fʀᴏᴍ ꜰɪʀsᴛ ɢʀᴀᴅᴇ, and during all my school years, I was known by class-mates and teachers as Cat Cobb. Both my parents were devoted to their cats, most of whom were strays that I rescued, but my relationship to cats goes beyond devotion. It's a commitment. They are part of me, and I am part of them, and that's how it has been all of my life. A hungry or suffering stray is not bearable to me. I am compelled to help them whenever and wherever I can. Was I a cat in my past life . . . or is all this simply a rehearsal for becoming a cat in my next life?

Emily Cobb with Bobby and Miel

No one would have doubted that the little kid who brought home every street cat she could find to "make better" would become a breeder and cat lover for the rest of her life.

Joyce Gutches and Geronimo

MAGIC is a reminder of all the things that matter the most to me.

ALEX, about three months old in this photo, was one of the friendliest lions hand-raised by the staff at the Wild Life Safari in Winston, Oregon. Usually by the time the lions got this big they became unpredictable or too hard to handle, but not Alex! Kids could climb all over him and he would just purr.

The lions were kept in a huge pen surrounded by a moat. The pride consisted of ten or twelve who lived and bred freely in fairly natural surroundings. When babies were born they had to be removed and hand-raised, or the other lions would kill them. When they became too large to handle, they were put into a pen with other hand-raised lions and an old male who was a particularly good baby-sitter.

When the trainer came to purchase Alex, she was amazed when my boss walked right into the pen and called him, nearly full grown by then, and he came bounding up to her full of love and affection. Normally lions revert quickly to their predator instincts and are likely to want to have you for breakfast.

Alex was rare and a privilege to have known.

PHOTO: Wild Life Safari Photo

Margy Best and Alex

MAX LOVES PEOPLE, especially his mother (me). Being a very sociable and mellow boy, he enjoys his days with the neighbors when I am at work, but when I am home he is ecstatic and rarely leaves my side.

Nancy Kruger and Max

My name is Marguerite. I have also been called Maggie, Margie, Rita, Margret, and Margaret. I was born in Switzerland and became a U.S. citizen in 1930. After performing with horses as a circus rider in this country, I suffered an accident which put a stop to that career. Another severe accident gave me time to find myself, to feel more deeply about many things, one of which was that animals were often in need of help. I learned by observation — I found cats and kitties abandoned in parks, behind markets, on highways nowhere near habitation, in the heat of summer with no water, and I saw much worse. So I chose to help them because they cannot speak for themselves. I have been a volunteer with the Pet Assistance Foundation of Los Angeles since the summer of 1958.

There are several cats living with me. Having several cats in one household requires great diplomacy. Take jealousy, for instance. To avoid this, lie to your cats. If one is very special, you can give him or her special hugs while the others are asleep. Just be sure to tell each one, "You know very well I love you more than any other cat in the whole wide world!"

Marguerite Poley and Tina

I THINK CATS came here from outer space. On their old planet, they were the big shots. They had jobs and cars and houses; they had careers and took vacations and complained about taxes. Then, one day, one overworked, underpaid cat said, *"Enough! Let's blow this nip stand!"* and they got in their kitty spaceships and searched until they found the perfect world: Earth. Here humans welcome them into their homes, feed them, pet them, buy them cat toys, let them sleep all day, and love them for the amazing, mysterious creatures they are.

I look at Mini and see the possibility of all this in her eyes, and I think, "Who's the pet here?" She'll never tell.

PHOTO: Paul Rogoshewski

Liz Brahm and Mini

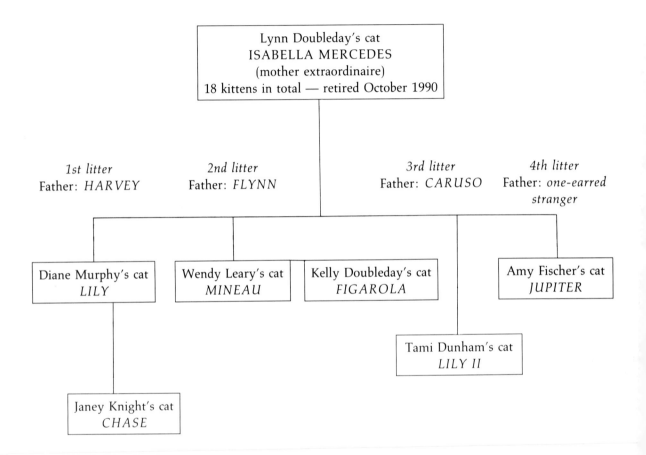

Lynn Doubleday's cat
ISABELLA MERCEDES
(mother extraordinaire)
18 kittens in total — retired October 1990

1st litter
Father: *HARVEY*

2nd litter
Father: *FLYNN*

3rd litter
Father: *CARUSO*

4th litter
Father: *one-earred stranger*

Diane Murphy's cat
LILY

Wendy Leary's cat
MINEAU

Kelly Doubleday's cat
FIGAROLA

Amy Fischer's cat
JUPITER

Tami Dunham's cat
LILY II

Janey Knight's cat
CHASE

Maine Coon Cats and Their Maine Women

*Clockwise from front left: Janey Knight and Chase,
Tami Dunham and Lily II, Lynn Doubleday and Bella,
Wendy Leary and Mineau, Amy Fischer and Jupiter,
Diane Murphy and Lily, Kelly Doubleday and Figarola*

PHOTO: Peggy McKenna

SIXTEEN YEARS OLD and thin as a rake. Toothless, torn, and tattered. Scabs from winter frostbite still clung to his bent and broken ears. Matted fur. People in the alley called him Scruffy. Too feral and street smart to be caught, he was too sick and weak to run when I finally found him. I took him home . . .

. . . and named him Oliver. After nine months of love and care, he's still toothless and tattered. And his ears are still bent and broken — but not his spirit. When he plays with my two younger cats, his kitten antics belie his days as a Dickensian street tough. Every day I hold him like this, look in his eyes, and tell him he's a precious little miracle. Maybe someday he'll believe me.

PHOTO: Jim Avis

Cheryl Lichak and Oliver

NOVEMBER 1989: Rats! Double rats! Why did Mom have to bring her home? She's barely two months old but acts like she owns the place. Although I continue to give her the cold shoulder, she spends most of her days trying to entice me into wrestling with her. That purr box of hers sounds like she's wired to an amplifier.

March 1990: Phoenix has now surpassed even my large girth. Mom has been feeding us generous helpings of food. She was afraid the kitten's growth would be stunted because I was hoarding all of the food in a sinister effort to bring Phoenix to an early demise. Was she ever wrong! Even the vet dubbed Phoenix Miss Piggy. Mom, however, was not amused.

May 1990: My sister, the delinquent. What a thief she is. Phoenix steals socks and even money (quarters mostly). She picks them up in her mouth and, looking totally ridiculous, runs to deposit the hot items in the corner room. I am much more intelligent. I steal food. I can even manage to remove toast from the toaster before Mom gets to it.

July 1990: Phoenix has been exhibiting more strange behavior. She laps the water from Mom's legs after she gets out of the shower, and Mom seems to find this endearing. Phoenix also has a tendency, when cleaning herself, to forget to put her tongue back into her mouth.

August 1990: That Phoenix has no sense of balance. I know how to maneuver to the top of the clothes-drying rack, whereupon Mom nicknames me "Nadia Comaneci." Meanwhile, Phoenix has slipped into the toilet on three separate occasions.

October 1990: We have moved into a real house with plenty of space to roam, inside and outside. I love our new home. I can stalk through the wild grass, climb trees, and bask in the sunshine. And Phoenix is quite safe, remaining indoors with her choice of rooms to run through. Mom now has a nice big bed, so that during those cold winter nights, both of us can keep her warm. And we purr contentedly . . . as long as Phoenix remains on her side of the bed!

PHOTO: Roni Epstein   *Claudia Zuckerman with Catalina and Phoenix*

My name is Mohammed Ali, but my mistress calls me Lee. I got a tough name 'cause I had to be. You see, before I was rescued and came here to live, I was an abused kitty. My first eight lives were terrible. They tied my legs together and threw me down a flight of stairs. For the last seven years, though, my ninth life has been paradise. I am the lord and master of three dogs, three humans, and thirty acres. At night I curl up at Donna's feet. When I want to go out for a midnight stroll to check on my property, I just walk up over her head, put my nose and long whiskers right in her eye, and meow! I wonder why she always laughs when I do that?

Photo: Jacqueline S. Walker

Donna Walker and Lee

I THINK the Animal Rescue League of Boston must be the beginning of many happy stories. I went there looking for a tabby kitten with a face like a lion. I said to myself, as I went down Chandler Street, "I'll get a male and I'll name him Leo." From the cage marked "Male," I picked out the one with the wildest eyes. He was scrapping with another kitten. "This is a male, right?" I said, as I filled out the papers, trying to hold Leo to my shoulder with one hand. The woman behind me remarked, "Some cats and their people just look like they belong together." Three weeks later, I brought Leo back for his booster shots. The veterinarian looked at the name on the card and hesitated before he asked, "Do you know that this is a female?" Leo loves to surprise people. That was her first surprise.

PHOTO: © Frank Siteman 1991

Amy Rebecca Kaufman and Leo

I THINK she's sweet and furry and kinda sneaky. She steals my Barbie dolls and drags them down the stairs. I like her very much. I love her because she's my little kitty. She's my Yankee Doll.

PHOTO: Martha Everson

Jeannie Beebe-Hubert and Yankee Doll

I WASN'T LOOKING for a cat, especially not two cats. My Eli, a solid silver gray male, had died a year prior of leukemia. Remaining home with me was Olive, a shy black-and-white female.

I remember that clear summer night. I was driving on a lonely country road in Connecticut. In the distance I saw a kitten in the middle of the road grooming itself. As I stopped the car to say hello and scold this careless kitty, I heard a lot of cat crying. I opened the door and, to my surprise, in jumped twin gray-and-white kittens. They were starving and quite hysterical. I decided to take them to my destination, feed them, and return them to their owners. As I watched these six-month-old kitties eat, leaving barely a crumb of food, I began to wonder if anyone missed them. The next day, they were mine. That was eight years ago.

They are a dynamic duo and very attached to each other. They brought my fourteen-year-old Olive out of her shell, and she even gets to chase Polka once in a while. The twins have filled out over the years. No one would know they had a tough time of it in their younger days.

Linda Serafin with Polka and Dot